MEXICO

...in Pictures

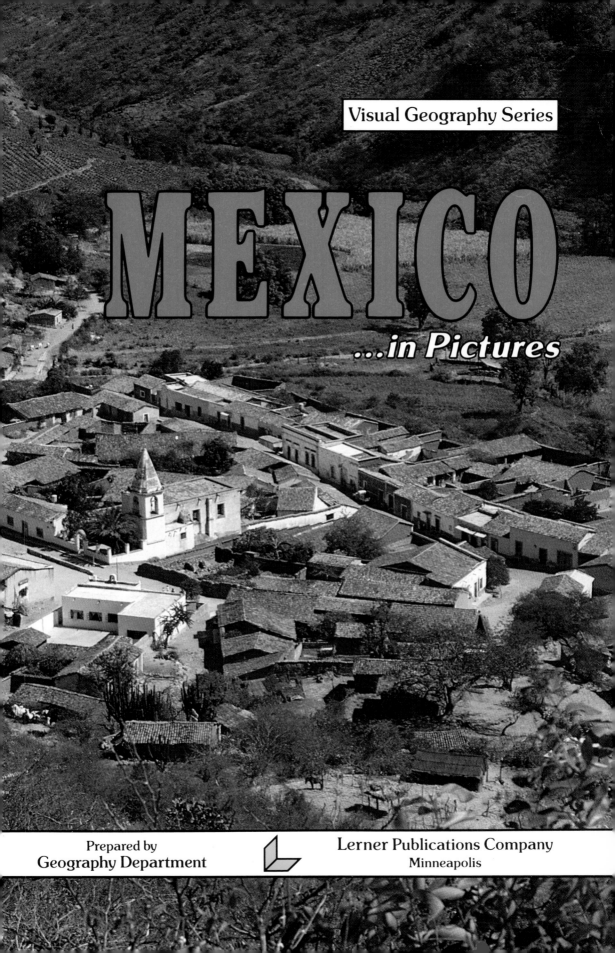

Visual Geography Series

MEXICO

...in Pictures

Prepared by
Geography Department

Lerner Publications Company
Minneapolis

Independent Picture Service

Bullfights begin with the colorful *paseo de las cuadrillas* — the parade of the matadors, picadors, and attendants.

This is an all-new edition of the Visual Geography Series. Previous editions have been published by Sterling Publishing Company, New York City, and some of the original textual information has been retained. New photographs, maps, charts, captions, and updated information have been added. The text has been entirely reset in 10/12 Century Textbook.

LIBRARY OF CONGRESS CATALOGING-IN-PUBLICATION DATA

Mexico in pictures

(Visual geography series)
Rev. ed. of: Mexico in pictures / prepared by Barbara J. Hall.
Includes index.
Summary: A brief introduction to the history, land, people, economy, and government of Mexico.
1. Mexico. [1. Mexico]   I. Hall, Barbara J. Mexico in pictures.   II. Lerner Publications Company. Geography Dept.   III. Series.
F1208.M585 1987   972   86-15234
ISBN 0-8225-1801-5 (lib. bdg.)

International Standard Book Number: 0-8225-1801-5
Library of Congress Catalog Card Number: 86-15234

VISUAL GEOGRAPHY SERIES

Publisher
Harry Jonas Lerner
Associate Publisher
Nancy M. Campbell
Executive Series Editor
Lawrence J. Zwier
Assistant Series Editor
Mary M. Rodgers
Editorial Assistant
Nora W. Kniskern
Illustrations Editor
Nathan A. Haverstock
Consultants/Contributors
Dr. Ruth F. Hale
Nathan A. Haverstock
Sandra K. Davis
Designer
Jim Simondet
Cartographer
Carol F. Barrett
Indexer
Kristine S. Schubert
Computer Systems Consultant
Rhona H. Landsman
Production Manager
Richard J. Hannah

Courtesy of Minneapolis Public Library and Information Center

Diego Rivera's sculpture-painting, which tells the story of Mexican sport, adorns the Olympic Stadium in University City.

Acknowledgments

Title page photo courtesy of Dr. Ruth Hale.

Elevation contours adapted from *The Times Atlas of the World*, seventh comprehensive edition (New York: Times Books, 1985).

1 2 3 4 5 6 7 8 9 10 96 95 94 93 92 91 90 89 88 87

Just two blocks from the Zócalo—Mexico City's gigantic downtown square—an old man shades his eyes to view part of the wreckage from the massive earthquake that hit the area late in 1985. Like this parking ramp, many modern structures collapsed, whereas some of the older churches and monuments resisted the forceful tremors.

Photo by Dr. Roma Hoff

Contents

Introduction **7**

1) The Land **10**
Physical Features. Flora and Fauna. Climate. Natural Resources.

2) History and Government **21**
Mexico Before Conquest. The Spanish Conquest. Mexican Independence. Modern Mexico Emerges. The Government.

3) The People **42**
Food. Art and Architecture.

4) The Economy **54**
Agriculture. Mining. Industry. Tourism. Future Prospects.

Index **64**

UNITED STATES

Tijuana

Nogales

BAJA CALIF. NORTE

TERR. DEL SUR

SONORA

CHIHUAHUA

Rio Grande

COAHUILA

SINALOA

DURANGO

ZACATECAS

Durango

Mazatlán

Monterrey
Matamoros

NUEVO LEON

SAN LUIS POTOSI

TAMAULIPAS

Lake of Tamiahua

NAYARIT

AGS.

GUANA JUATO

QRO.

HID.

PACIFIC OCEAN

Guadalajara

Puerto Vallarta

JALISCO

L. Chapala

L. Cuitzeo

MICHOACAN

L. Pátzcuaro

MEXICO CITY

D.F.

MEX.

MOR.

TLAX.

PUEBLA

Teotihuacán

Cuernavaca

COL.

GULF OF MEXICO

Bay of Campeche

Mérida

YUCATAN

Uxmal

Chichén-Itzá

QUINTANA ROO

CAMPECHE

Veracruz

VERACRUZ

TABASCO

Acapulco

GUERRERO

OAXACA

Pan-American Highway

CHIAPAS

BELIZE

GUATEMALA

HON

EL SALVADOR

N

MEXICO

State Boundaries

0 — 300 Miles

0 — 300 Kilometers

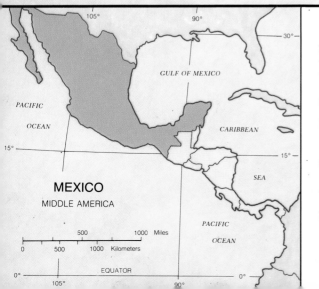

105°

90°

30°

GULF OF MEXICO

PACIFIC OCEAN

CARIBBEAN

15°

15°

SEA

MEXICO

MIDDLE AMERICA

PACIFIC OCEAN

500 — 1000 Miles

0 — 500 — 1000 Kilometers

EQUATOR

0°

0°

105°

90°

Colorful lights illuminate the Juárez Monument in Mexico City. This great white marble semicircle was erected in memory of Benito Juárez, the poor Indian shepherd who became Mexico's great defender of the oppressed.

Introduction

The republic of Mexico, officially the United Mexican States, is a populous, resource-rich nation struggling against forces beyond its control. Plummeting oil prices, devastating earthquakes, and a turbulent history have left their marks on Mexico, but they have not suppressed the Mexican spirit. Mexicans are the inheritors of one of the Western Hemisphere's richest cultural traditions – a blend of Spanish and Indian ways that may be the source of Mexico's resilient optimism. And Mexico has a lot to be optimistic about: mineral resources of staggering size and variety, a growing industrial capacity, and a modern political stability that seems almost miraculous in light of the nation's stormy past.

7

The diversity that distinguishes Mexico owes much to the Mexican knack for reaching for the future with one hand while preserving the best from the past with the other. In Mexico's cities, broad modern plazas lead to ancient Aztec temples, traffic-jammed streets are just minutes away from narrow pack trails, and baseball and bullfights vie for the attention of crowds. Tourists jet in for a sunny vacation beside the awe-inspiring remnants of mighty pre-Columbian Indian civilizations. Elaborate churches rise from the foundations of pagan temples, and broad highways follow the Indian trails along which the conquistadors marched.

Mexico's oil-drilling rigs suggest a recurring Mexican lesson: that a supposed godsend can turn out to be a tragic disappointment. Just as Cortés was not the god some Aztecs are said to have mistaken him for, oil was not the economic savior in the 1970s that it seemed to be. Mexico's rumbling volcanoes suggest yet another lesson: that the geologic forces at work beneath Mexico are extreme. As the disastrous Mexico City earthquake of 1985 showed, Mexico's greatest challenge may lie in adapting to forces it cannot control while harnessing those it can.

Independent Picture Service

The civilizations of the ancient Indians and the conquering Spaniards have mingled and blended so that today Mexico is a fascinating land of contrasts. Tula, the great capital of the ancient Toltec Indians, is the site of many majestic statues that once served as supports for temple entrances.

Courtesy of Minneapolis Public Library and Information Center

The beautiful coastal resort of Acapulco on the Pacific coast is a favorite vacation spot. Here, luxurious hotels and fine restaurants compete for the tourist trade, deep-sea fishing attracts anglers from all over the world, and the sunset has been called the most magnificent in all Mexico.

Seen from the air, Mexico City's Bull Ring (*front*) and stadium seem to dominate the city. Said to be the largest in the world—it seats 60,000—the Bull Ring hosts loyal and enthusiastic spectators, some of whom attend every fight. The bullfight, often depicted in sculpture and in other art forms, today competes with baseball for the public fancy.

Spectacular mountains rising to 9,000 feet and forests reflecting abundant rainfall cover much of Chiapas State along the Pacific coast in southern Mexico.

1) The Land

Mexico is a land of great physical and cultural diversity. With an area of more than 750,000 square miles, it is approximately one-fourth the size of the continental United States (exclusive of Alaska).

Mexico is usually not considered to be part of Central America. On the north is the United States, and the famous Rio Grande of song and story forms part of the border between the two countries. The Gulf of Mexico and the Caribbean Sea bound Mexico on the east, Guatemala and Belize bound it on the south, and the Pacific Ocean is on the west. The peninsula of Yucatán in eastern Mexico helps divide the Atlantic into the Gulf of Mexico and the Caribbean Sea. Baja California, or Lower California, is a peninsula jutting southward from the state of California.

Mexico is a federal republic divided into 29 states, 2 territories, and the Federal District of Mexico, which encompasses Mexico City. When Mexicans speak of "Mexico," they mean Mexico City; they refer to the country as a whole as "the republic."

Physical Features

Much of Mexico is mountainous. Two great mountain chains, the Sierra Madre Occidental and the Sierra Madre Oriental, extend along Mexico's west and east coasts, respectively. A number of valleys and plateaus of differing altitudes lie among these mountains. The Central Plateau, Mexico's topographical heartland, is located between these two ranges. This plateau comprises more than half of Mexico's land area. From north to south, the Central Plateau gradually rises in altitude from about 3,600 feet near the U.S. border to about 8,000 feet in some of the southern intermountain basins. Most of the principal cities are located on this plateau, and here the density of population is greatest, especially in the sections near Mexico City. It is also the chief agricultural region.

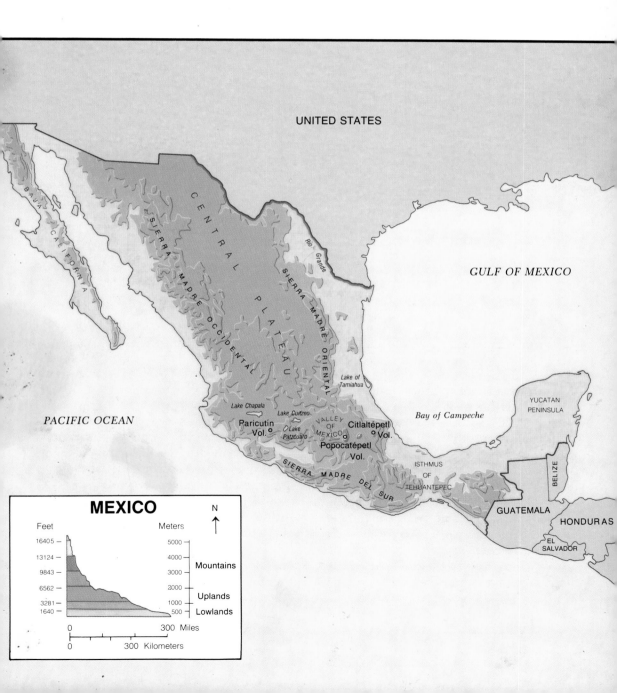

The majestic peak of the volcano Popocatépetl – an Aztec name for smoking mountain – rises more than 17,000 feet above Mexico City. Before the Spanish conquest, Popocatépetl and Ixtaccíhuatl (white woman) – the slightly smaller volcano next to it – were thought of as gods. According to Indian legend, Popocatépetl – a great Aztec warrior – was in love with the beautiful princess Ixtaccíhuatl. When he went off to fight the enemies of the Aztecs, his rivals told the princess that he had been killed, and she pined away. When Popocatépetl returned from battle to find his beloved was dead, he built a great pyramid to hold her and placed himself nearby to guard her through eternity.

A number of high volcanic peaks rise above the southern part of the Central Plateau. Mexico's two highest peaks, Citaltépetl (or Orizaba) and Popocatépetl are both of volcanic origin. Paricutín first erupted in 1943, and volcanic ash and hardened lava now cover its surrounding territory for many miles. Mexico's newest and most recently active volcano, El Chichon, exploded in 1981, killing 2,000 people. South of this volcanic zone are jumbled masses of mountains and the Sierra Madre del Sur, which make southern Mexico one of the most inaccessible, picturesque, and undeveloped parts of the country.

Mexico's rugged mountains have created tremendous problems in the areas of transportation and communication. Many sections of the republic are almost impossible to reach, and they have remained economically and culturally undeveloped.

Low tropical plains lie along both of Mexico's coasts. These are broadest along the Bay of Campeche, a southern extension of the Gulf of Mexico. The Yucatán Peninsula, which defines the eastern side of the bay, is composed almost entirely of flat lowlands, and a strip of low country crosses the Isthmus of Tehuantepec from this bay to the Pacific Ocean.

Popocatépetl has not erupted since 1702, but occasionally it emits vast clouds of smoke.

There are many rivers in Mexico, but few are navigable. Although the Rio Grande forms more than 1,000 miles of the border between the United States and Mexico, it is useless for navigation during most of the year. The rivers are valuable, however, as sources of water power and irrigation. Of Mexico's few lakes, Lake Chapala, southeast of the city of Guadalajara, is the largest. Lake Pátzcuaro and Lake Cuitzeo in Michoacán and the Lake of Tamiahua in Veracruz are known for their scenic settings.

Divers perform on Sundays for a small donation at this waterfall, located just west of San Antón, a potters' village.

13

Mexico's campesinos, or peasant farm laborers, often devise clever means of survival—as illustrated by this fence of living cacti that were arranged for penning goats, near Mitla.

Sunsets along the Pacific Ocean are exquisite, as here, near the port city of Guaymas.

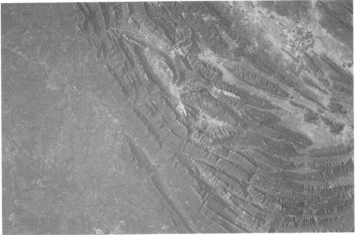

This view, taken by U.S. astronauts aboard a space shuttle, shows a portion of the Sierra Madre Oriental in the vicinity of the city of Monterrey. Note the clarity of the ridge and valley structures—as seen from the vantage point of space—and (at lower left) the transition to the desert environment of Mexico's Central Plateau.

Intensely brilliant bougainvillea enhances this hotel courtyard in the Yucatán.

Flora and Fauna

The range of Mexico's flora is wide—from tropical palms on the coasts, through temperate-zone species on the plateaus, to low-growing alpine herbs and shrubs on the high mountain slopes.

Wildlife includes such large mammals as the tapir, jaguar, cougar, wild sheep, pronghorn, deer, and bear. Many smaller species—monkeys, rodents, armadillos, opossums, reptiles, birds, and insects—thrive in the varied habitats of Mexico.

These monkeys live on *Isla de Changos*, "Island of Monkeys"—a special preserve located in Lake Catemaco, southeast of and inland from the port of Veracruz.

Climate

North Americans think of Mexico as very hot, but this is not true throughout the country. Because of the varying altitudes and because the country lies partly in the temperate zone and partly in the tropical zone, its climate ranges from tropical to cool. There are two seasons: it is rainy from June to October and dry from November to May. The rainfall, like the temperature, varies considerably with the altitude. The low country along the coasts, on the Yucatán Peninsula, and on the Isthmus of Tehuantepec is humid, while semi-arid highland plains cover much of the north. The average temperature of the plateau region is from 60° to 70° F, and on the coastal plains it ranges from 80° to 90° F.

Independent Picture Service

The rivers of the Yucután Peninsula flow underground beneath a limestone plateau. In places called cenotes, pits have formed where the limestone has caved in and made wells. This lithograph of a sepia watercolor by Frederick Catherwood shows people coming to draw water at the well at Bolonchén in the 1840s.

Independent Picture Service

Cactus grows everywhere in Mexico. Indians in isolated villages eat its fruit and make a dessert from the fleshy stems, and their most popular drink is pulque, made from the fermented juice of the maguey cactus. Tequila and mescal are also made from the maguey. On these sun-baked rocks (*above*) from which a few hardy cacti sprout, large but harmless lizards warm themselves.

Independent Picture Service

Independent Picture Service

As it has for centuries, a giant ahuehuete stands in a churchyard near Oaxaca. Its huge limbs and enormous trunk (160 feet in circumference) have provided shade and shelter for countless Indians, missionaries, and soldiers.

Independent Picture Service

Independent Picture Service

Mexico's rugged mountains, which are continuations of ranges in the United States and Canada, have long been the source of rich mineral deposits. In the past, these mountains isolated many sections of the country. Now this has changed, and tiny villages clustered on mountainsides and nestling in valleys are linked to the rest of the republic by a railway that crosses the Sierra Madre Occidental. The railway connects the farmlands on the Pacific coast with the wheat and cattle regions of the northern plains. At the same time, it has opened a new tourist path across the wild, almost-unexplored range of mountains.

Natural Resources

Some regions of Mexico are covered with forests. Tree varieties range from pine and oak to valuable hardwoods and dyewoods. Mexico has set aside nearly 50 forests as national parks, in addition to several national forest reserves.

What was true when the conquistadors came to exploit Mexico's wealth is still true today: Mexico has some of the richest mineral deposits in the world. Mineral extraction is the most highly developed and best-organized industry in the nation. By the 1980s, oil had become as important a product as the more traditional metallic mineral exports. A great zone of metallic mineral deposits lies within the Sierra Madre Occidental. Nearly every state, however, has some mines.

17

Courtesy of Minneapolis Public Library and Information Center

Independent Picture Service

Picturesque Taxco, "the city with a silver lining," has been a mining town since the sixteenth century. The handsome church that dominates the town was built by Joseph Le Borde, called José de la Borda, a Frenchman who came to Mexico in the early 1700s to make his fortune. He more than succeeded, and as a thanks-offering for his good luck he had the magnificent twin-towered church built in 1757.

Mexico has long been one of the world's leading producers of silver, zinc, lead, antimony, and manganese, a relatively scarce metal used in making high-quality steels. Other important minerals are sulfur, iron, gold, copper, molybdenum, arsenic, bismuth, cadmium, mercury, tungsten, and tin. The nation is known to have large reserves of uranium, coal, and natural gas, as well as oil.

Courtesy of Leanne Hogie

The Barranca del Cobre — or Copper Ravine — in the Sierra Madre Occidental holds a vast wealth of mineral deposits.

Courtesy of Jon Poll

North of Mexico City, near the archaeological site of Tula, the lands of the Valley of Mexico look worn-out — the result of over-farming, deforestation, and erosion — all caused by people over thousands of years.

Hardy and colorful, croton grows profusely in Mexico.

Courtesy of Sylvia Johnson

Guadalajara, with more than two million people, is Mexico's second largest city and the capital of the state of Jalisco. At more than 5,000 feet above sea level, it has a dry, mild climate.

Courtesy of Dr. Ruth Hale

Guanajuato is a mining town dwarfed by the great mountain La Bufa. Two miles outside the town is La Valenciana mine. Centuries ago, at the height of its production, La Valenciana was the richest mine in the world. Its total output was estimated to be worth 800 million pesos.

The rocky land near Teotihuacán offers little pasture for grazing sheep.

The hacienda where this courtyard is located was constructed in the early sixteenth century, soon after the Spanish conquest. Now restored and converted for use as a hotel, the early architecture graces the town of Vista Hermosa in the state of Morelos.

2) History and Government

Mexican history can be seen in terms of four distinct periods. The first includes the many centuries before Columbus set sail for the New World, during which highly organized and sophisticated Indian civilizations flourished in the Mexican plains and valleys. All this came to an end with the arrival of the Spanish in 1519, which ushered in the second period of Mexican history. For almost 300 years, *Nueva España* (New Spain), as the country was called, was ruled by Spaniards who sent the vast wealth they found back to their motherland, cruelly exploited the natives, and brought widespread unrest. The third period, that of Mexican independence, began in 1810 when the discontented populace broke forth in rebellion—the first of many uprisings against corrupt and apathetic governments. It was not until 1910, however, that Mexico had a social revolution that truly freed it from centuries-old bonds and allowed it to enter the present period in its history—that of modern democracy.

Mexico Before Conquest

Hundreds of years before the arrival of the Europeans, Mexico was an active fount of civilization. From prehistoric times to the coming of the Spaniards, Mexico was inhabited by a succession of peoples with differing languages, customs, and degrees of culture. First one group then another was supreme, leaving behind evidence of highly developed societies where crops were planted, rich fabrics were woven, and houses and palaces were built of stone and mortar.

The grimacing face on this Olmec boulder may represent a long-dead ruler of a civilization that flourished three thousand years ago.

THE OLMECS

Long ignored by archaeologists in spite of the colossal sculptured heads they left, the Olmecs are now regarded as the forerunners of all the higher Mexican civilizations. Discoveries based on radiocarbon dating have placed the beginning of the Olmec culture in the thirteenth century B.C. in the coastal lowlands along the Gulf of Mexico near modern Veracruz. The Olmec civilization came to a mysterious end about the first century B.C., but its traces have been found in all subsequent cultures of the area.

THE MAYA

One of the greatest of these cultures was that of the Maya, who first appeared in present-day Guatemala, Honduras, and southeastern Mexico. One of the earliest

A crouching figure decorates an example of the archeological remains of the Olmecs in La Venta park.

Courtesy of Jon Poll

Courtesy of Mexican National Tourist Council

Palenque, located in southeast Mexico, was once a thriving and populous Mayan community. The site consists of 15 miles of ruins of which only a small fraction have been excavated. The area was abandoned by the Maya about A.D. 800. Among the exquisite ruins at Palenque are a great palace and a high watchtower. The builders at this Mayan site used plaster to obtain a smooth finish on the stone, which is a practice somewhat different from the tooled-limestone method more often seen in Mayan architecture.

Courtesy of Dr. Ruth Hale

Huge stone pillars are part of the Mayan ruins at Chichén-Itzá in southeastern Mexico. A well-preserved chacmool (*right forefront*) peers out into space, like an immovable guard. Life-sized sculpted stone figures associated with the rain god, chacmools are often found located at the entrance to temples.

Temple ruins of the late Mayan period (roughly A.D. 1200) are also plentiful at Uxmal. Both Chichén-Itzá and Uxmal are in the Yucatán Peninsula, where the Mayan civilization was centered at the time of the arrival of the Spanish.

dates found to have been recorded in the Americas—November 4, 291 B.C.—was found on a Mayan altar.

By the tenth century, the Maya had abandoned their remarkable cities in the south and migrated to the Yucatán Peninsula. Here their culture reappeared during the tenth and twelfth centuries, attaining the peak of its development by 1100. Elaborate cities were built in Chichén-Itzá and Uxmal (pronounced oosh-MAL), and even today the evidence of their achievements astounds archaeologists and casual visitors. Primarily an agricultural people, the Maya excelled in art, architecture, mathematics, and the measurement of time. In astronomy they surpassed the Egyptians and Babylonians, and they developed a remarkable calendar and a system of hieroglyphic writing.

The Mayan Empire fell early in the twelfth century, principally because of tribal wars. When the Spanish conquerors swept through the area, they ruthlessly destroyed what was left of the Mayan

An ancient Mayan ball court in Monte Albán, Oaxaca State, was once the site of a game that resembled modern-day basketball. The two opposing teams bounced a ball through a hoop while supportive spectators cheered from the bleachers.

cities. Still, the descendants of the original Maya might have been able to rebuild these cities if the region had not been wracked by a devastating hurricane and a series of plagues that killed tens of thousands shortly after the Spanish onslaught.

Monte Albán was also the religious home of the Zapotec Indians. The city is famous for its tombs, tunnels, plazas, and large stone carvings. This example shows dancing figures and symbolic devices carved in low relief.

Dominating the extensive ruins at Teotihuacán, the splendid Pyramid of the Sun is over 200 feet high. The sides are terraced, and wide stairs lead to its summit.

A temple at Chichén-Itzá has a single chamber and entrance, decorated with an ornate frieze.

The human figure depicted in this Mayan carving is adorned with an elaborate headdress and jewelry.

This jade mosaic death mask—from Pacal's tomb in Palenque—was stolen from the National Museum of Anthropology in December 1985.

The Maya decorated some of their buildings profusely, as evidenced by the ornate work at the Chichén-Itzá site.

TEOTIHUACAN AND THE TOLTECS

Years before the Christian era, the area around Mexico City was inhabited by Indians of a cultured race of unknown origin. The land where these people lived was called Teotihuacán, "the place where gods are made." There they erected two great pyramids, the Pyramid of the Moon and the Pyramid of the Sun. These magnificent pyramids were used not as burying grounds but as temples of worship, astrological observatories, and military fortresses. The work on them—and on the great temple of Quetzalcóatl built some centuries later—was all done by hand, the stones being held together by mortar made with a mixture of lime, sand, clay, and ground corn.

Teotihuacán fell around A.D. 650, and a race known as the Toltecs moved into the area around A.D. 900. They were master craftspeople, builders of imposing cities, skilled farmers, and accomplished weavers. Their system of military, political, social, and religious laws was quite complex. Toltec attacks on the Mayan cities in Yucatán contributed to the downfall of that empire, but during the eleventh century the Toltecs were themselves overrun by another group, the Chichimecs.

Intricately carved images of the Feathered Serpent adorn the temple of Quetzalcóatl.

Courtesy of Minneapolis Public Library and Information Center

Quetzalcóatl was a god who endured through many Indian civilizations. Colossal stairs lead up the sides of the temple dedicated to his worship, and religious festivities were probably celebrated on the platforms of variegated stone. (Courtesy of Minneapolis Public Library and Information Center)

28

Teotihuacán was abandoned long before the Aztecs arrived in the area, yet the ruins still stand today as awesome monuments of a remarkable culture.

Near Veracruz is the Pyramid of the Niches in El Tajín, built about A.D. 600. Once part of an extensive city, the great pyramid is made of volcanic rock and adobe, stuccoed in various hues. The four sides of the pyramid represent the four seasons, and its 365 niches symbolize the days of the year.

The modern-day Mexican artist Diego Rivera chose to paint the ancient Aztec market at Tlatelolco. The bustling market was a source of amazement to the Spanish conquistadors who remarked on the volume of trade and the orderliness with which commerce was conducted. In the upper right corner, the central square of Tenochtitlán can be identified by its several tall pyramids.

THE AZTECS

Although few early records exist, we know that in about A.D. 1325 the wandering Aztecs arrived at the site of present-day Mexico City. It was there, according to legend, that they saw an eagle perched on a cactus and holding a serpent in its claws. Interpreting this as a sign from the gods to settle down, they constructed their capital city, which they called Tenochtitlán. Today the eagle and serpent form

Mexico's national emblem, appearing on its coins and stamps.

The Aztecs built their first houses on wooden pilings driven into the bottom of a shallow lake, and they laid out their gardens in the mud. Gradually, however, they erected an elegant city with handsome temples and palaces, impressive public buildings, busy marketplaces, and efficient canals. Two centuries later the invading Spaniards recorded that Tenochtitlán was even more beautiful than Venice, then the loveliest city in Europe.

The Aztecs were apparently the first to domesticate the turkey, which was unknown in Europe until the Spaniards brought it back from the New World. The Aztecs contributed much to Mexico as well, including the country's name, which was derived from *Mexica*—the name the Aztecs used for their tribe.

The Aztecs, like the Maya, had a remarkably accurate calendar and a complex religion. One of the many Aztec gods, Quetzalcóatl—whom the Aztecs "inherited" from the earlier civilizations of the Toltecs and Maya—was honored as the creator god of learning and culture. Lord of the wind and air, Quetzalcóatl is symbolized as a feathered serpent, and many representations of him can be seen throughout Mexico.

By carefully and deeply etching the stone, Aztec sculptors imitated fur on a carved figure of a coyote.

This image of the goddess Coatlicue—mother of the war god—stands over eight feet high.

The Aztecs were a warlike people whose empire, at the time of the Spanish conquest, extended over much of central and southern Mexico. A nation of warriors and merchants, they came into contact with numerous other tribes in the area. The Aztecs, with their rich and varied customs, had absorbed much from earlier civilizations and from contemporary Indians whom they dominated. Frequent clashes among various groups resulted in an interchange of customs, language, myths, and agricultural techniques. Of the many contributions the Aztecs made to this exchange, the most important was probably their expertise in social organization and government.

The Spanish Conquest

When the Spanish conquistadors arrived in Mexico in 1519, they found a huge land with some areas heavily populated and other sections almost uninhabited. The Aztecs were the dominant group, and their emperor, Montezuma II, ruled from Tenochtitlán in the Valley of Mexico. There were, in all, about 4.5 million Indians scattered throughout the country.

Two years earlier, in 1517, Francisco Fernández de Córdoba had made an exploratory foray from Cuba. In 1518 a second expedition, with Juan de Grijalba at its head, arrived for a look around and encountered resistance from the Indians. Hernán Cortés was originally chosen by the Cuban governor, Diego Velázquez, to lead a third expedition. However, by the time Cortés set sail in February 1519, the governor had changed his mind and wished to replace him; his journey took place without official approval. Nevertheless, Cortés arrived in a fleet of 11 vessels—with 600 men, 17 horses, and 10

Hernán Cortés cut short a university career to seek his fortune in the New World. He was seconded to Diego Velázquez, governor of Cuba, and set sail for Mexico against Velázquez's orders.

cannons. Had he not been a man of indomitable will—a born leader who could demand and get the impossible from his followers—his attempt at conquest would surely have failed, for the Aztec army of 200,000 warriors outnumbered the Spaniards by about 350 to 1. Yet after landing in Mexico Cortés burned his ships to convince his men that they had to succeed—or die.

There are conflicting versions of Cortés's reception at the Aztec capital of Tenochtitlán. According to one report, Montezuma at first welcomed the invading force, believing that a prophecy had come true and that Quetzalcóatl, the revered god, had at last returned to rule. Another record states that the Aztec emperor, frightened by omens, tried to prevent Cortés and his men from advancing inland.

Whatever Montezuma's attitude toward the Spanish, Cortés was eventually invited into Tenochtitlán as a guest of the emperor. But Cortés was uncomfortable surrounded by thousands of potentially hostile Aztecs and, in a brassy move, decided to ensure his own safety by taking Montezuma hostage. It worked. Cortés placed Montezuma under a sort of house arrest in the emperor's own palace.

After a brief time, Cortés received word that nine Spanish ships were anchored in the Caribbean off Veracruz. These ships were part of a mission from Governor Velázquez in Cuba, who had decided that it was time to assert his authority over Cortés. Cortés left one of his lieutenants, Pedro de Alvarado, in charge of Tenochtitlán and went to meet the governor's expedition. After defeating the leader of this expedition in a brief battle, Cortés added his would-be captor's forces to his own army.

While Cortés was meeting that challenge, Alvarado was in trouble in Tenochtitlán. Afraid that the Aztecs were mounting a revolt, Alvarado and his forces attacked a religious gathering of nobles and killed about 200 Aztecs. Following

Cortés was determined to conquer the Aztecs, and several historical accounts report that he was aided in doing so by an Aztec prophecy. The prophecy held that the exiled god Quetzalcóatl would return to rule the empire. At first, then—mistaken to be the returning god and his followers—Cortés and his men were welcomed by Emperor Montezuma with the honor and respect due to a god.

this massacre, the Spaniards were trapped in their own barracks, unable to get out of the city and besieged by the angry citizens of Tenochtitlán.

When Cortés heard about Alvarado's difficulty, he made a forced march back to the city. The army marching with Cortés now included a number of recruits from among the Tlaxcalans, a neighboring group of Indians who were unfriendly to the Aztecs. Cortés was permitted to enter Tenochtitlán, but this was just a trap. The Spaniards were soon under attack by wave after wave of Aztecs seeking revenge. Having reentered Montezuma's palace, Cortés once again held the emperor hostage, and the Spanish forced Montezuma to plead with the Aztecs to stop fighting and to let the Spaniards leave the city. Probably by accident, Montezuma was hit by a stone while he was trying to calm the populace. He died soon afterward.

The Spanish eventually fought their way out of Tenochtitlán, but the battle was fierce and hundreds of Cortés's men were killed in flight. The Aztecs rejoiced in their victory and appointed a new emperor, but he was soon felled by smallpox, a disease introduced by the Spanish. This brought to the throne the last of the Aztec emperors, a nephew of Montezuma named Cuauhtémoc.

Cortés, after having fled not only Tenochtitlán but the Valley of Mexico as well, returned for his last assault on the city. He encountered stiff resistance from Cuauhtémoc's forces and then set up a siege to prevent food and water from getting to the Aztecs in Tenochtitlán. After three months, the Aztecs were too weak to resist the final Spanish onslaught in August 1521. Cuauhtémoc was captured, and the Spanish tortured him in an effort to find out where he had hidden the great treasures of Tenochtitlán—which the Spanish knew to exist but which they were unable to find after capturing the city. Cuauhtémoc held fast, and legend has it the treasure remains hidden even today.

Having conquered Tenochtitlán, the Spanish proceeded to destroy the magnificent pyramids, temples, and palaces and to rebuild the city for themselves. Then, with forces bolstered by 40,000 Tlaxcalans, the conquerors continued their ruthless domination and destruction in other parts of the country. Yet when Cortés returned to Spain in 1528 expecting a victor's welcome, he found that King Charles I had been turned against him, and the greatest of the Spanish conquistadors spent his last years a disappointed and neglected man.

In 1535 New Spain became a viceroyalty—a status that gave it a resident ruler acting on behalf of the king—and the process of Christianizing and Europeanizing the Indians went on. But the Spanish were few compared to the natives, and establishing control over all of New Spain was a matter of centuries.

Slowly the population developed into three distinct groups: the whites, the mestizos (people of mixed Spanish and Indian descent), and the Indians. The Roman Catholic Church was all-powerful, owning most of the land, whereas the Indians who tilled the soil and worked the mines were

The conquest of Mexico by the Spanish was bloody, and battles with Aztec warriors were waged over several months. After Tenochtitlán, the Aztec capital city, was captured, it was razed to the ground and became the foundation of Mexico City.

The Spanish brought their lifestyle, language, religion, and artistic influences to the New World. An indigenous artist, Baltasar de Echave Ibía, made a study in blue of the Mexican landscape soon after the conquest in the sixteenth century.

virtual slaves. Although there was much legislation to improve the lot of the Indian, oppression continued. Even after Indians were declared legally free and black slaves had been imported to provide a work force, the Indians remained serfs, obligated to pay tribute and provide personal service to the landholders. All the country's vast wealth was sent to Spain; nothing was left for the people who produced it.

Over the centuries, conditions worsened, with an added complication. The mestizos were numerically strong, but socially, economically, and politically they had no position and no privileges. There was also great antagonism between the Spanish-born whites (*gachupines*) and the native-born whites (*criollos*). Discontentment with Spanish rule grew, and from across the ocean came news of French revolutionary ideas. It was time for Mexico to enter its third period—independence—and the opportunity came when Napoleon defeated Spain in 1808.

The Jesuits, founded by Saint Ignatius of Loyola (*above*), were very influential in the colonial period of Mexico's history.

35

Mexican Independence

A humble parish priest, Miguel Hidalgo y Costilla, launched the Mexican people's rebellion on September 16, 1810. From his pulpit in the town of Dolores, about 120 miles northwest of Mexico City, Hidalgo issued a call to Mexicans to cast aside gachupín rule. This was the signal for armies to spring up. Thus began a campaign of liberation, which soon changed from small local revolts to a widespread uprising of the oppressed.

Hidalgo led a constantly growing but badly organized army of 80,000 against some 7,000 Spanish troops. Eventually, a rivalry among the rebel leaders weakened their organization. Hidalgo's forces did gain several victories in battles with the Spanish royalists, but, in 1811, the Father of Mexican Independence was defeated and executed. The patriotic cause was then taken up by another priest, José María Morelos y Pavón, who declared Mexico's independence anew and drafted a constitution. But Morelos too was executed for his efforts on behalf of Mexican independence.

Courtesy of Museum of Modern Art of Latin America

Father Miguel Hidalgo y Costilla, Mexican priest and revolutionary, figures in a mural by one of Mexico's most celebrated artists, Diego Rivera. Hidalgo, who is remembered as the Father of Mexican Independence, instigated one of the first uprisings from his hometown pulpit in Dolores.

Independent Picture Service

Another major figure in Mexico's efforts to gain independence was José María Morelos y Pavón, whose commemorative statue towers above the island of Janitzio.

The revolution almost died away, but guerrilla attacks continued until 1821, when Agustín de Iturbide, appointed by the viceroy to quell the uprisings, instead joined forces with the revolutionists. He drew up the Plan of Iguala, which included a guarantee of independence, preferably under a monarchy. General Iturbide was named Emperor Agustín I of Mexico in July 1822, but his reign was a brief one. At the end of the year, the republican leaders Antonio López de Santa Anna and Manuel Félix Fernández (Guadalupe) Victoria drove the new emperor out and proclaimed Mexico a republic. During Iturbide's reign, the Central American states of El Salvador, Nicaragua, Guatemala, Honduras, and Costa Rica were annexed by Mexico, but with the collapse of the empire they regained their independence.

It was the sad fate of the Mexican republic to be at the mercy of dictators for many years. Officials of the new republic

Chapultepec Castle was built over a vanquished Aztec fortress in 1783 and became the home of the viceroys of New Spain. It later became the imperial residence of the ill-fated Emperor Maximilian and today houses a national museum.

were out for personal gain, and nothing was done to solve the land problem or to eliminate other social evils. The most prominent figure during the early days of Mexico's republic was Santa Anna.

General Iturbide became Emperor Agustín I in 1822 and built this opulent residence, where he lived until his demise in 1823. Surrounded by twentieth-century buildings, Iturbide Palace is now the head office of a bank.

A detail from a mural painted by José Clemente Orozco depicts Benito Juárez, a Zapotec Indian, who is revered by Mexicans as the man who saved the nation from foreign occupation. He was also a reformer who worked for social justice in the nineteenth century.

Treacherous, greedy, conceited, and incompetent, he controlled Mexican politics from 1833, when he was first elected president, to 1855, when the intense dislike of the Mexican people for his dictatorial rule forced him to resign. Four times during his domination of Mexico he was forced out; four times he seized power again. It was during his dictatorship that Texas broke away from Mexico and the disastrous war with the United States inflicted on Mexico the painful loss of what is now New Mexico, Arizona, and part of California.

In 1857, two years after Santa Anna's downfall, a new constitution was drawn up, providing for a more democratic and liberal government. With Santa Anna out for good, power passed to a totally different kind of man.

Benito Juárez, a full-blooded Indian who became president in 1858, had managed against overwhelming odds to receive an excellent education. A lawyer and man of scholarly tastes, he was an austere patriot—scrupulously honest and passionately determined to improve the lot of the Indians. Yet during his administration civil war broke out because of opposition, led by conservative landowners and the clergy, to the new constitution.

Juárez and his supporters defeated the opposition, but further trouble was ahead. The conservatives had sought foreign aid, and they found it in Napoleon III of France, who sent a French army of occupation to Mexico. Without bothering to consult the Mexicans, Napoleon selected the Austrian archduke Maximilian to be emperor of Mexico. Maximilian, a mild and tolerant man who was eager to found a democratic state, thought the Mexicans truly wanted him, but he and his wife Carlota were greatly disillusioned by their reception when they arrived in Mexico City in June 1864.

Juárez, forced into exile, carried on guerrilla warfare against the French. During this time the United States was embroiled in its own Civil War, but once that war was over the U.S. government invoked the Monroe Doctrine and insisted on the departure of the French troops. Deserted by Napoleon, Maximilian was captured by Juárez's troops and executed in 1867. The empire came to an end and Juárez governed until 1872.

Modern Mexico Emerges

In 1877, Porfirio Díaz, one of Juárez's generals, was elected to the presidency. Reelected in 1884, Díaz remained the head of the government, except for one short period, until he was overthrown by the revolution of 1910. A cynical and subtle man, he was autocratic but also extraordinarily energetic and capable. His administration brought an era of unprecedented peace and prosperity to Mexico. There were great material developments, with the spread of railways, an increase in foreign investments, and steady growth in

The Mexican National Palace runs the length of one side of Zócalo square. Built on the site of Montezuma's palace, the residence once housed Mexico's presidents but is now largely devoted to government departments.

national wealth. Manufacturing and agriculture flourished, and the capital was cleaned up and modernized.

Nonetheless, Mexico still had serious economic and social problems that grew worse instead of better. Díaz's administration stifled democratic institutions, increased the misery of the Indians by taking away their ancestral lands, and made all-too-obliging concessions to foreign corporations. Roads were poor, schools were completely inadequate, child labor was common, and living conditions were miserable—except for the privileged classes.

Finally, opposition to the evils of Díaz's political system brought about the Mexican Revolution in 1910. Francisco Madero, an idealistic, humanitarian member

The twentieth century has witnessed the rise of drug production in Mexico. The output of a poppy field—one of many throughout the country—will eventually be used to make opium. Opium is the source of the illegal narcotic, heroin. According to U.S. intelligence sources, many Mexican officials of the modern era have become involved in the lucrative drug business.

39

of a rich landowning family, provided the impetus for the revolution. When support for Madero became strong even in the vicinity of Mexico City, Díaz resigned and departed for Paris. Madero became president, but he disappointed many of his former supporters and was assassinated before he could stabilize the government.

Revolutionary factions in various parts of the country again took arms, and one of the most turbulent periods in Mexico's history followed. Among the picturesque leaders who assembled private armies in those troubled times were Francisco (Pancho) Villa, a bandit chieftain, and Emíliano Zapata, who hoped to restore to the Indians their ancient heritage.

During this garish era of glittering promises and monstrous betrayals, three Mexican presidents were assassinated— as was Zapata. One incident after another strained relations between Mexico and the United States, and more than once the two countries were on the brink of war. Things began to look better in 1917, when Venustiano Carranza became head of the Mexican government. He drew up a new constitution, restating more vigorously the principles outlined in the constitution Juárez had drawn up in 1857. It provided for freedom of worship, divided the large landed estates, declared the nation owner of natural resources, and confiscated all Church property. This document, amended several times, has endured as the basis of the Mexican government to the present day.

In 1934, General Lázaro Cárdenas was elected president, and so began an era in which solid achievements replaced wild speeches. Immediately after taking office, Cárdenas put into operation a six-year plan for economic, social, and educational reform. In the first four years of his administration, more land was distributed to the peasants than had been distributed in all the years since the revolution. The new policy for Mexico included irrigation projects, dams, power plants, and the estab-

lishment of agricultural training stations. An extensive scheme to build modern roads and railways was inaugurated to unify the country. In 1938, Cárdenas took over the oil fields, which had been leased and operated by foreign companies for decades. Mexico had at last emerged into the twentieth century.

War was declared on Germany, Italy, and Japan in May 1942, and many Mexicans saw action. In addition, Mexico's abundant supplies of strategic war materials were of invaluable aid to the Allied cause.

Since achieving stable government early in the twentieth century, Mexico has made significant social and political advances. Private ownership of property is guaranteed, education is compulsory, monopolies are forbidden, and workers are protected. Government efforts to improve such basic services as health care and housing have

Courtesy of Library of Congress

General Lázaro Cárdenas, Mexico's president from 1934 to 1938, is credited with economic, social, and educational reforms.

Many "tent cities" sprang up after Mexico City's devastating earthquake of 1985 because tenants from the condemned housing projects wanted to stay close to their belongings.

done much to raise the national standard of living. However, the nation's deep indebtedness—made worse by falling oil prices in the mid-1980s and by continued high rates of population increase—drains the economy of development capital and jeopardizes Mexico's position in international trade. Another major blow was the earthquake that struck the Mexico City area on September 19, 1985. A colossal disaster in human terms—8,000 people dead, 30,000 wounded, hospital beds reduced by 70 percent—it was also a major economic setback, inflicting damage estimated at some $4 billion.

The Government

Mexico, like the United States, has a federal system of government. Executive power is vested in the president, elected by direct popular vote. One difference between the Mexican and U.S. systems is that the Mexican president serves a six-year term and may not be reelected. There is no vice-president. If the president dies or is disabled during the first three years of the term, a new election is held, and if the office is vacated during the last three years, the congress elects a successor.

Legislative power is vested in a congress consisting of two houses—the Senate and the Chamber of Deputies. In the upper house there are two senators from each state and two from the Federal District (the area around Mexico City), each elected to a six-year term. The Chamber of Deputies is composed of one representative for every 250,000 inhabitants of each state, elected for a term of three years. Each member of each house has an elected alternate, who takes the legislator's place in case of absence or death.

The highest tribunal in Mexico's judiciary branch of government is the Supreme Court of Justice. This body consists of 21 members who are appointed to full-time positions by the president and confirmed in them by the Senate. At the regional level, there are circuit and district courts to handle cases involving infractions of district or local laws.

Like the federal government, each of Mexico's state governments is composed of three branches—executive, legislative, and judicial. The executive branch is headed by a popularly elected governor who serves a six-year term. Each state has a one-house legislature that drafts state laws and approves budgets for each *municipio*—a unit of local government roughly comparable to a U.S. county—within the state. A state's judicial system includes lower courts and a state supreme court to which the decisions of lower courts may be appealed.

41

Courtesy of Dr. Ruth Hale

Indian markets, like this one at Pátzcuaro, are held weekly in many Mexican cities and villages. Buying and selling provide opportunities for meeting and visiting, important aspects of Mexican life.

3) The People

Mexico's population is large and growing. In 1985, the population of Mexico was estimated at 80 million. According to some estimates, by the year 2100 Mexico could have as many as 195 million people and could be the tenth most populous country in the world. The central area of the country, especially in and around Mexico City, is the most densely populated. The population of the Federal District, which includes Mexico City, nearly doubled between 1974 and 1986 and stands now at more than 15 million people, making it one of the largest urban areas in the Western Hemisphere. The movement of people away from traditionally agricultural areas to the large cities reflects the number of former agricultural workers now involved in industry and trade. Only about one-third of the Mexican people still live in rural areas.

Mexico's second largest city is Guadalajara, which has a large cotton and wool industry and is the capital of the state of Jalisco. The third largest, Monterrey, is the capital of the state of Nuevo León and is often called the Mexican Pittsburgh because of its many steelworks. There are 50 cities with populations of more than 100,000.

The Mexican people are usually thought of in terms of three major racial groups. Indians, who account for 29 percent of the population, are directly descended from the original inhabitants. Generally, they are poor and they live in rural areas—often the same areas settled by their ancestors thousands of years ago. Some of them are beginning to move to the outskirts of the cities, where they often congregate in neighborhoods of substandard housing.

There are at least 56 different Indian groups, each with its own language and culture.

At the opposite end of the socioeconomic scale are the Spaniards or "white" Mexicans, who are descended from Spanish conquerors and colonists and who make up about 6 percent of the population. They dominate the upper social classes but are sometimes described as haughty and too conscious of their aristocratic heritage—often with little public recognition of how reduced their circumstances may have become.

The largest group, about 55 percent of the population, is made up of the mestizos. This group gives Mexico much of its charm and gaiety, its laughter and guitar music, and its relaxed philosophy of *mañana,* or traditional tardiness. The remaining 10 percent of the population is made up of various other peoples.

Mexicans of pure Spanish descent have traditionally been the wealthiest people, while the mestizos have made up the masses of poor workers. Most of the pure-blooded Indians have hardly been touched by the twentieth century. They speak their own languages rather than Spanish, and their way of life differs little from what it has been for centuries. The government's education programs, however, are slowly bringing them in touch with more modern customs.

Because of the isolation of the Indians and the unsanitary conditions in which

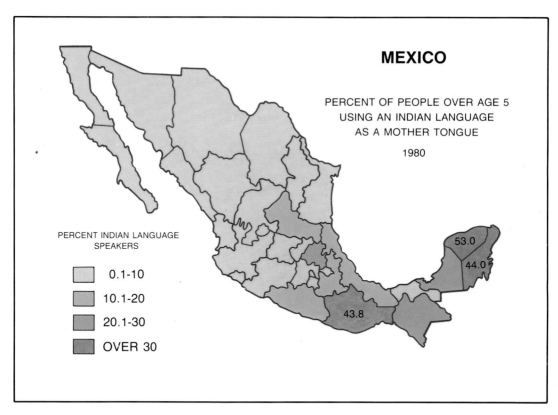

This map shows the percentage of people over five years old whose native tongue is an Indian language. The data is mapped by state; in states with percentages over 30, the actual percentage figure is shown. Note the concentration of states with medium and high values in the southeast part of the country. Data from *Censo General de Población y Vivienda, 1980,* for the United Mexican States.

There are still some remote villages where Indians speak only the dialect of their ancestors. Many do not care to be photographed, for a superstition holds that the camera catches and keeps their souls. Others willingly pose, showing off their prized possessions.

they lived, disease had taken a heavy toll. At one time, the shortage of doctors willing to live in remote areas made the situation seem hopeless. In 1936, however, the federal government instituted a project whereby every Mexican citizen studying medicine must practice in some rural area for five months immediately before receiving a medical degree. This requirement led to the improvement of rural sanitary conditions, and, although there is still much to be done, great progress has been made.

Since 1944 the government has waged war against illiteracy—with remarkable results. The program's slogan, "Each One

Teach One," summarized its unusual approach: Every literate man and woman was compelled by law to teach an illiterate person or contribute to a literacy center. Night schools were created, and special schools for the rural population were set up, stressing practical programs suitable to the students' needs. Instead of forcing the Spanish language on the non-Spanish-speaking Indians, the government wisely decided to help them become literate in their own languages. This strategy has been most effective, for once the Indians found the value of reading in their native languages, many became eager to learn Spanish too. As a result, they are being integrated into the community without being asked to give up their Indian identities. By 1985, 83 percent of the Mexican people were literate.

Children at a rural grade school are hard at work on a classroom exercise. At this age children generally do all their school work in a single notebook, something that they often prize later on in life. (Courtesy of Inter-American Development Bank)

A festival is usually going on somewhere in Mexico. In Papantla de Olarte, Veracruz—home of the Totonac Indians—the fiestas are among the most beautiful in the country.

Independent Picture Service

Elaborately costumed for the Dance of the Fishermen, young boys rest at Lake Pátzcuaro's shore.

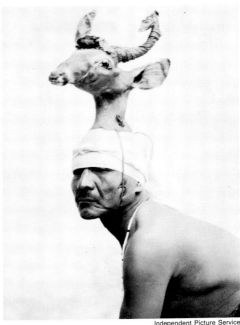

Independent Picture Service

Accompanied by primitive music, Yaqui Indians of Sonora perform the ancient deer dance at their fiestas.

Courtesy of Minneapolis Public Library and Information Center

Mexico is famous for its colorful basket weaving.

Photo by Dr. Roma Hoff

Mexico, unfortunately, still has many beggars, young and old — like this woman at the side door of the Cathedral of Mexico.

The beautiful beach at Cancún is one of Mexico's many tourist attractions. Tourism along the coasts provided Mexico with 90 percent of its earnings from foreign exchange before the oil boom of the 1970s.

Courtesy of David Mangurian

Courtesy of Jon Poll

The mountains run into the sea along much of Mexico's Pacific coastline, providing a colorful backdrop for tourists choosing to camp along the water.

Food

The diet of the average Mexican today is very similar to that of his or her Aztec forebears, its basics being maize (corn), beans, and hot chili peppers. Some of the most popular foods in modern Mexico—tortillas, tamales, and *pozole* (a kind of corn chowder), for example—date from Aztec days. Tortillas, a versatile staple of the Mexican diet, are the flat cornbread rounds that form the shells of tacos and enchiladas. Tamales, like enchiladas, contain a spiced filling (usually meat) inside a soft cornmeal shell, but the cornmeal dough of a tamale's shell is not formed into a tortilla; instead, the unbaked dough is shaped into oblongs that encase the filling, and the tamales themselves are then wrapped in cornhusks and steamed.

Some Mexican dishes are now widely enjoyed in other countries, especially in the United States. Tacos, chili con carne, enchiladas, and guacamole are a few of the Mexican favorites that are now almost as familiar in Minneapolis as they are in Monterrey.

Courtesy of The Creative Kitchens of Lawry's Foods, Inc.

Mexican rice and tacos, now popular worldwide, are nutritious and versatile Mexican foods.

Independent Picture Service

An Ocotlán mother carries her child in a secure sling fashioned from her *rebozo,* or shawl.

Independent Picture Service

The peel of a fruit makes a hat for this grinning boy.

48

A feature of Mexican small-town life is the open-air market. Here people of the surrounding countryside bring their fruit, vegetables, blankets, and pottery to sell or barter. Market day is also a social occasion, and there is often a small orchestra to add to the gaiety.

Although the Spaniards introduced the European wine grape, Mexicans consume far less wine than beer and pulque, which is the fermented juice of the maguey cactus. A very strong native drink derived from the maguey is tequila, which has become quite popular in other countries, principally the United States. Less well known abroad is mescal, also made from the maguey cactus. Mexican beers are of excellent quality and today are an important export item.

The cathedral at Guadalajara (*above*) closely duplicates Gothic architecture, while the mosaic tiles in the courtyard of the convent at Santa Mónica (*right*) borrow from Indian motifs.

Art and Architecture

When the Spaniards arrived in Mexico, they found civilizations that astounded them. In pre-Columbian Mexico, there were buildings of amazing beauty as well as ritual masks, mural paintings, jewels, pottery, and sculpture of equally remarkable craftsmanship. There were monumental statues, delicate featherwork mosaics, and tiny figured masks of jade, turquoise, and rock crystal.

During the colonial period, architecture was the major mode of artistic expression. Indian craftspersons, under the direction of the Spaniards, superimposed Indian motifs and details on European styles, creating rich, complicated forms. Sculpture of the early colonial period was European in subject matter, but the technique and some ornamentation were Indian. Most sculpture had a religious theme, with startlingly realistic saints and crucifixions represented in stone and wood. Gold was worked with exquisite skill, and craftspersons of this period also produced ornamental pieces in wrought iron and finely carved furniture.

Photo by Dr. Roma Hoff

Young women in traditional dress gather to promenade on a Sunday afternoon in Guadalajara's new mall, Plaza Tapatío. The plaza comprises squares, monuments, fountains, and the Cabañas Museum, which houses the art work of native son, José Clemente Orozco.

Mexico has been called the land of handicrafts. From Aztec and colonial days to the present, various districts have been known for their distinctive traditional products, and the Mexican Indian has been a master craftsperson. Mexico's beautifully decorated and glazed ceramics and exquisite silver jewelry are known all over the world. Other typical items for which the country is famous are textiles—especially the colorful serapes—tooled leather, glassware, carved and painted wooden masks, lacquered bowls and trays, basketry, and *retablos* (religious drawings).

Courtesy of Minneapolis Public Library and Information Center

Courtesy of Minneapolis Public Library and Information Center

Mexico is known for its handicrafts. These trays have been lacquered in colorful, stylized patterns, adding beauty to functional objects.

The Church of Fray Pedro de Gante in Texcoco combines Indian and European styles of architecture.

An ornate facade in Guanajuato depicts religious themes.

Perhaps Mexico's greatest contribution to world art is mural painting. The great masters include Diego Rivera, José Clemente Orozco, David Alfaro Siqueiros, and Rufino Tamayo. Their work, supported by the government, appears in many public buildings, including some in the United States. Vivid in hue and often violent in subject matter, Mexican paintings frequently have been instruments in political and social propaganda.

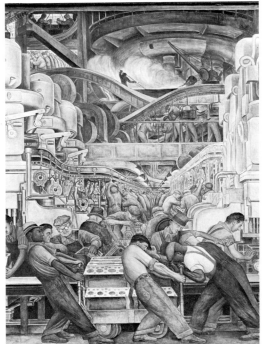

A detail (*above*) from a mural by Rivera depicts the production and assembly of motors. Man's control of the universe through technology is a common theme for Rivera. Packed with symbols of modern industrial society, this mural expresses the oppression and depersonalization of human values. The mural depicting Indians at work (*right*), also by Rivera, is in Cortés's palace in Cuernavaca.

Independent Picture Service

The university library is faced with colored mosaics by Juan O'Gorman depicting the history of ideas. Surveying the scene is a statue of Miguel Alemán, Mexico's president from 1946 to 1952.

The choice of Mexico City as the site of the 1968 Olympic Games spurred the building of new facilities, notably those in the University City section of the capital. The Olympic Stadium, with a capacity of 80,000 people, boasts murals by Diego Rivera. Another feature is the absence of staircases—all approaches to the various levels are by tunnel or ramp. The stadium provides a splendid setting for events such as the opening and closing ceremonies of the olympiad. (Independent Picture Service)

Yellow safflower in the Pacific lowlands is harvested from huge, irrigated fields where cooperatives use modern farming techniques. The safflower will be made into oil and dye.

4) The Economy

Agriculture

With its great mineral wealth and increasing industrialization, Mexico is no longer primarily an agricultural country. Today, fewer than 40 percent of the working people are engaged in farming. Much of Mexico's land area cannot be used for agriculture because of high mountains or extreme dryness. The most productive farming areas are the Caribbean coast, the central and southern portions of the Central Plateau, and the northwest coastal plain.

Maize and wheat, the staple grains of the Mexican diet, are the most important food crops, and—thanks to improved seeds and farming techniques—the country has become self-sufficient in these two crops. Maize is cultivated in all parts of Mexico, but the growing of wheat is restricted mainly to the Central Plateau. Other significant food crops are beans, chick-peas, rice, oats, and barley.

The chief commercial crops are coffee, cotton, sugar, and henequen (or sisal)—a fibrous material derived from agave plants and used in making twine. Mexico is one of the world's largest coffee producers. Coffee makes up almost 30 percent of the total value of Mexico's agricultural exports each year. The coastal states of Veracruz, Oaxaca, and Chiapas are the chief coffee-growing areas, although there are also some inland coffee plantations.

Coffee must be picked by hand because no machine can distinguish between the green "cherries" and the ripe red fruit. After the harvest, the coffee cherries are cleaned, dried, hulled, and graded according to size before sending them to market.

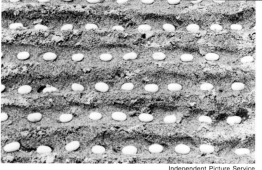

In the Yucatán, sisal stalks are gathered in bundles (*right*) along the roadsides. After the cream-colored sisal fibers have been extracted at a Yucatán factory, a donkey-pulled train car (*below*) hauls away waste pulp. The fibers are hung on racks to dry before being twisted into rope and twine. (Courtesy of Dr. Ruth Hale)

Mounted on horseback, Joel López Córdoba oversees a herd of brahma cattle near Cárdenas in Tabasco State. The Mexican government has invested heavily in developing this sparsely inhabited area to attract settlers from other regions of the country.

Cotton is grown primarily on the northern Central Plateau in the states of Durango and Coahuila. It accounts for almost 20 percent of Mexico's agricultural exports. Other important agricultural products include chicle, tobacco, citrus fruits, and vegetables.

In addition to crops, cattle are very important to Mexican agriculture. Cattle are raised chiefly in the north, along the U.S. border.

José Adolfo León Pacheco (*left*), a government agronomist, explains to Julián Arias Rodrigues how to achieve better water circulation in this field of irrigated rice at an *ejido,* or communal farm. Estimates indicate that more than one-third of Mexico's total farmland is now irrigated.

Yoked oxen are still used to till fields, but more up-to-date agricultural methods are gradually being adopted.

56

Uneven distribution of land was one of the basic causes of the wars and revolutions that swept Mexico through much of its history. At the time of the 1910 revolution, less than 10 percent of the total population owned land. The general system was that of the hacienda—a self-contained, almost self-governing unit on which almost all the necessities of life were produced. One of the most significant results of the revolution was Mexico's transition from a land of vast estates to one of many small tracts owned by individual farmers or worked cooperatively.

Some of these cooperative units, known as *ejidos,* have been especially successful. In the northwest states of Sonora and Sinaloa, millions of acres of agricultural land have been developed along the coastal plain. Water for irrigation is supplied by reservoirs on the rivers that descend from the Sierra Madre Occidental. This region has become a leading source of Mexico's cotton and wheat. Tomatoes, melons, peas, beans, cucumbers, peppers, and eggplant grow rapidly and are shipped northward where they compete with the winter vegetables and fruit of California, Florida, and Texas.

Courtesy of Inter-American Development Bank

The Ignacio Allende Dam, named for a hero of Mexico's struggle for independence, is located in mountainous Guanajuato State.

Because sugarcane takes 11 months to ripen, fields at various stages of ripeness are found near each other in the Sierra Madre Occidental and will be harvested at different times. Surrounding mountain slopes are covered with drought-resistant vegetation, which is occasionally used for grazing.

Courtesy of Dr. Ruth Hale

Mining

Since the Spanish conquest, minerals have traditionally been Mexico's greatest source of wealth. Up until the last few decades, however, the exploitation of Mexico's minerals brought little benefit to the Mexicans themselves. The Spaniards virtually enslaved the Indian population, put them to work in the mines, and robbed Mexico of its mineral riches, especially silver.

Although Mexico's mountains are economic obstacles in many ways, they are also a source of great wealth, for most of the country's metal ores lie buried in the mountains. The chief metallic minerals are silver, lead, and zinc, but gold, copper, sulfur, cadmium, and other minerals are

Independent Picture Service

The giant kettles of a lead refinery in Monterrey are tended day and night.

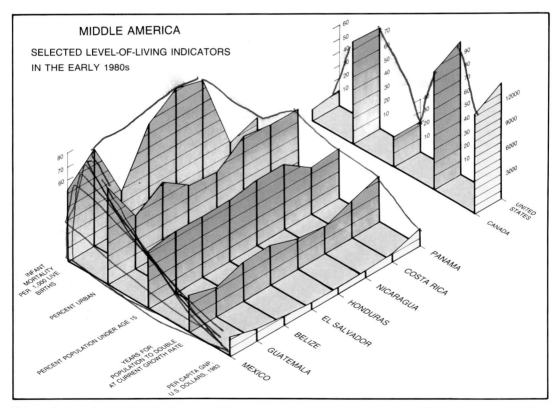

This graph shows how each of five factors, which are suggestive of the quality and style of life, varies among the eight Middle American countries. Canada and the United States are included for comparison. Data from "1986 World Population Data Sheet" (Washington, D.C.: Population Reference Bureau, Inc., 1986).

Oceangoing trawlers are under construction at Mazatlán, a port on Mexico's Pacific coast. The boats are owned by locally based fishing cooperatives, which use them to catch shrimp and sardines.

plentiful. Most of Mexico's mineral production is for export, partly because the country's domestic economy is not yet sufficiently developed to consume it. The exceptions are coal and iron, which are used by Mexican factories.

Petroleum is one of Mexico's most valuable resources. Foreign investors, mainly British and American, were the first to develop and industrialize Mexico's petroleum reserves on a large scale. What seemed at the time to be extraordinarily large reserves were discovered, and Mexico became, in the early twentieth century, the world's second largest producer of petroleum. Since the late 1920s, petroleum production has increased, but Mexico's proportionate share of the world market has declined because of the development of fields in other regions, notably the Middle East.

In 1939 the Mexican government nationalized the oil industry so that enormous profits would not continue to be taken out of the country. In the years since, Mexico has directed the development of its own oil reserves through a state-subsidized company, Petróleos Mexicanos (Pemex).

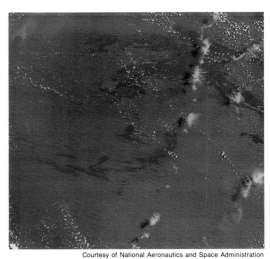

The dark patches on the beautiful waters of the Gulf of Mexico are oil, spilled in 1979 by a runaway well belonging to Petróleos Mexicanos, a Mexican petroleum company. The offshore well, known as Ixtoc #1, discharged 10,000 to 30,000 barrels of oil into the gulf per day until it was finally brought under control.

About 20,000 people – like these Veracruz fishermen who are preparing their nets for a day's outing – are engaged in Mexico's fishing industry.

By 1975, Mexico was benefiting from the worldwide oil boom. For some years before, Mexican oil fields had not been producing at their full capacity. However, the world oil crisis of 1973–1974 spurred renewed

Protexa, a South American company, manufactures fiberglass (used in the lining of oil pipes) and coal tar (used to surface highways). In developing its oil wealth, Mexico has established many new industries that manufacture oil industry equipment or that use oil in their production.

Mexican oil prospecting and production. Subsidies to Pemex were terminated in December 1974, and the government sharply raised the prices of petroleum and its by-products. These actions prompted Pemex to launch an unprecedented expansion scheme.

By 1983, Mexico was the world's fourth largest producer of oil—after the Soviet Union, the United States, and Saudi Arabia. It is believed to have over 7 percent of the world's petroleum reserves, or almost twice as much as the United States. In the early 1980s, it was exporting about half of its total yearly oil production, mostly to the United States.

The income that Mexico gained from oil exports was greatly reduced, however, when oil prices dropped sharply in the mid-1980s. In less than five months—from November 1985 to March 1986—the price of the average barrel of oil on world markets dropped from about $30 to about $14. Mexico thus faced the prospect of taking in less than half of what it had planned to earn from oil. This situation greatly complicated the country's already-severe debt problems and made many of its hopes for economic development more difficult to realize.

Industry

Industry has long been the slowest sector of the Mexican economy. However, like many of the industrially underdeveloped countries of the world, Mexico is making great efforts to expand its industrial production. These efforts began seriously in the 1930s and received great momentum during World War II, when the republic had difficulty obtaining imports from its usual sources. Many new light industries sprang up to fill the gap. Direct government investment has played a fairly small role in expanding industry; more important has been legislation designed to induce greater private investment. Mexico's chief industrial products are textiles, clothing, and processed food products.

Courtesy of Dr. Ruth Hale

Glassblowing, symbolic of Mexico's well-developed handicrafts industry, is a major economic activity in Tlaquepaque, near Guadalajara. Products made by hand in small-scale workshops often are sold in Mexican border towns and in import shops in the United States.

Courtesy of Inter-American Development Bank

Panlufas Imperial, a small company that manufactures shoes in Mexico City, is one of many new firms created as a result of the Mexican government's programs to promote new industries.

Courtesy of Inter-American Development Bank

The existence of a plentiful supply of labor and low wages has made Mexico a popular place for foreign-owned automobile companies to establish assembly plants. This assembly line at the Dina Auto Plant is part of an Italian company located in Mexico City.

Courtesy of Minneapolis Public Library and Information Center

Xochimilco (soh-chee-MEEL-koh), 15 miles southeast of Mexico City, is a popular excursion point for natives and tourists alike. The name means "land sown with flowers," and the beautiful floating gardens are often described as Mexico's Venice.

Tourism

Tourism remained a major source of national income—$4.4 billion in 1980. Mexico hopes to attract more than seven million tourists annually by 1990. Cancún on the Gulf of Mexico and Mazatlán, Puerto Vallarta, and Acapulco on the Pacific continue to attract thousands of tourists from all over the world, principally from the United States. Many U.S. tourists also visit Mexican cities like Tijuana, Matamoros, and Nogales, which lie just across the border from cities in the United States. Inland places such as Guadalajara (with nearby Lake Chapala), Cuernavaca, and Mérida, are also popular.

Courtesy of Minneapolis Public Library and Information Center

The breathtaking sweep of the bay, the vivid blue waters, and the gleaming luxury hotels have made Acapulco—viewed here from the coastal highway—a widely acclaimed resort.

Future Prospects

Although Mexico entered the 1970s with one of the soundest economies in Latin America, the country eventually found itself burdened with massive foreign debts and a growing trade deficit. People began to pour into the cities, and thousands attempted to cross the border in search of jobs in the United States. Some factors in the problem were a rapidly growing population and a chronic shortage of arable land. For a while, Mexico hoped that oil earnings would solve its financial problems, but oil has proved to be an undependable source of income and one that has tended to widen the gap between rich and poor.

By early 1986, Mexico's economy was in serious trouble. More than 50 percent of its earnings from exports were required to pay the interest on its national debt of more than $90 billion. Investment capital fled the country as industrialists were reluctant to sink money into the uncertain Mexican economy. The peso had been devalued so

Courtesy of U.S. Drug Enforcement Administration

Authorities of the United States and Mexico work together to eliminate the production of dangerous drugs. Here an airplane sprays crop-killing chemicals on drug-plant fields located in a hilly region along the Mexico–New Mexico border.

far that more than 700 pesos were needed to buy a single U.S. dollar. (Ten years earlier the exchange rate had been seven pesos to the dollar.) As of mid-1986, the Mexican government, the U.S. government, and Mexico's creditors were exploring ways to soften the impact of the oil-price decline on Mexico's already-weakened economy.

Tensions between the United States and Mexico rose in the mid-1980s as a result of increased drug smuggling. Illegal drugs—especially marijuana and cocaine—have long been sent across the border from Mexico to buyers in the United States, unlawfully bringing highly valued U.S. dollars into the Mexican economy. In 1986, representatives of the United States administration charged that corrupt Mexican officials were accepting bribes from the smugglers in exchange for turning a blind eye to cross-border drug traffic. Mexico denied that corruption was widespread and that Mexican officials were any more lenient with drug traffickers than were their U.S. counterparts.

Mexico faces considerable economic problems, but it also has considerable resources to use in tackling them. Especially if the price of oil rebounds, as many analysts expect, the difficult 1980s may become just an unpleasant footnote to the story of a vigorous Mexican economy.

Courtesy of U.S. Drug Enforcement Administration

The dried, milky juice of the poppy plant is used in making the narcotic drug, opium. The eradication of poppy fields thriving in Mexico would help to reduce drug production.

Index

Acapulco, 8, 62
Agriculture, 11, 14, 17, 19, 39–40, 42, 54–57
Alemán, Miguel, 53
Alvarado, Pedro de, 32–33
Archaeological ruins, 19, 21–29
Architecture, 8, 18, 37, 41, 50, 52–53. *See also* Indians, architecture
Armed conflicts, 32–34, 36–38. *See also* Mexican Revolution; World War II
Artists, 4, 30, 35, 52–53
Arts and crafts, 30, 35, 46, 49–53, 61. *See also* Indians, arts and crafts
Assassinations, 40
Aztecs, 8, 12, 29–34, 37
Baja California (Lower California), 10
Borda, José de la (Joseph Le Borde), 18
Bullfights, 4, 9
Campeche, Bay of, 12
Cancún, 47, 62
Cárdenas, Lázaro, 40
Caribbean Sea, 10, 32
Carlota (empress of Mexico), 38
Carranza, Venustiano, 40
Catemaco, Lake, 15
Cattle, 17, 56
Cenotes, 16
Central America, 10, 21, 37
Central Plateau, 11–12, 14, 54
Chacmool, 24
Chapala, Lake, 13, 62
Chapultepec Castle, 37
Charles I, King (of Spain), 34
Chiapas (state), 10, 54
Chichén-Itzá, 24, 26–27
Chichimecs, 28
Citlaltépetl, 12
Climate, 16, 19, 54
Coahuila (state), 56
Coastal plains, 12, 16–17, 54, 57
Coffee, 54–55
Congress, 41
Constitutions, 36, 38, 40
Copper Ravine (Barranca del Cobre), front cover, 18
Cortés, Hernán, 8, 32–34
Cortés's palace, 52
Cotton, 54, 56–57
Criollos, 35
Cuauhtémoc, 33–34
Cuba, 32
Cuernavaca, 52, 62
Cuitzeo, Lake, 13
Currency, 63
Dance, 46
Democracy, 21, 40–41
Díaz, Porfirio, 38–40
Dictators, 37–38
Dolores, 36
Drugs, illegal, 39, 63
Durango (state), 56
Earthquakes, 5, 7–8, 41
Economy, 8, 39–41, 48–49, 54–63
Education, 39, 40, 43–44
Ejidos, 56–57
Energy sources, 13, 18, 40, 57, 59

Exports, 54, 56–57, 60
Federal District of Mexico, 10, 41–42
Fernández de Córdoba, Francisco, 32
Festivals, 45–46
Fishing, 8, 59–60
Flora and fauna, 15–17, 19, 62
Food, 16, 48, 50
Foreign investments in Mexico, 38–39, 59–60, 63
Forests and parks, 10, 17, 19, 22
France, 38
Gauchupines, 35
Government
  arts support, 52
  buildings, 39
  corruption, 37–38, 40, 63
  economic reforms, 40, 61
  land reform, 40, 56–57
  nationalization of oil industry, 59–61
  social reform, 39–41, 44
  stability, 7, 40
  structure, 41
Grijalba, Juan de, 32
Guadalajara, 13, 19, 42, 50–51, 61–62
Guanajuato (city), 20, 52
Guanajuato (state), 57
Guatemala, 10, 22, 37
Gulf of Mexico, 10, 12, 22, 59, 62
Health, 40–41, 43–44
Hidalgo y Costilla, Miguel, 36
History
  independence, 21, 35–38
  modern era, 21, 38–41
  postconquest, 21, 32–35, 50
  pre-Columbian, 21–31, 50
Honduras, 22, 37
Housing, 40–42
Ignacio Allende Dam, 57
Ignatius of Loyola, Saint, 35
Illiteracy, 44
Indians, 8, 14, 16, 21–35, 38–40, 42–44, 50–52, 58. *See also* Tribes, Indian
  architecture, 21–30, 50, 52
  arts and crafts, 21–22, 24–28, 31, 50–51
  calendars, 24, 29, 31
  legends, 12, 28, 33, 44
Industry, 7, 17, 39, 42, 52, 54–55, 58–61
Irrigation, 13, 40, 54, 56–57
Island of Monkeys (*Isla de Changos*), 15
Iturbide, Agustín de, 37
Ixtaccíhuatl (volcano), 12
Jalisco (state), 19, 42
Juárez, Benito, 7, 38, 40
Lakes, 13, 15, 62
Languages, 21, 35, 43–44
La Valenciana (mine), 20
Madero, Francisco, 39–40
Maize, 48, 54
Mañana, 43
Maps and charts, 6, 11, 43, 58
Markets, 42, 49
Matamoros, 62
Maximilian (emperor of Mexico), 37–38
Maya, 22–28, 31

Mazatlán, 59, 62
Merida, 62
Mestizos, 34–35, 43
Mexican National Palace, 39
Mexican Revolution, 38–40
Mexico
  borders, 10, 13
  monarchy, 37
  name, origin of, 31
  national emblem, 30
  physical features, 11–14
  size, 10
Mexico City, 4, 5, 7–12, 19, 28, 30, 34, 36, 38–42, 48, 53, 61–62
Mexico, Valley of, 19, 32–33
Mexitli. *See* Huitzilopochtli
Michoacan (state), 13
Minerals, metals, and mining, 7, 17–18, 20, 50–51, 54, 58
Monroe Doctrine, 38
Monte Albán, 25
Monterrey, 14, 42
Montezuma II, 32–33, 39
Morelos y Pavón, José María, 36
Mountains, 10–12, 14, 17, 20, 47, 54, 57–58
Music, 43, 46, 49
Napoleon, 35
Napoleon III, 38
National debt, 41, 60–61, 63
Natural resources, 7, 17–18, 40, 63
New Spain (*Nueva España*), 21, 34, 37
Nogales, 62
Nuevo Léon (state), 42
Oaxaca (city), 17
Oaxaca (state), 25, 54
Oil, 7–8, 17–18, 40–41, 47, 59–60, 63
Olmecs, 22
Olympic Stadium, 4, 53
Orizaba. *See* Citlaltépetl
Orozco, José Clemente, 38, 51–52
Pacific Ocean, 10, 12, 14, 47, 59, 62
Palenque, 23
Paricutín (volcano), 12
Pátzcuaro Lake, 13, 46
People
  characteristics of, 7–8, 42–45, 49
  racial groups, 42–43
  standards of living, 39–44, 46
Petróleos Mexicanos (Pemex), 59–60
Plan of Iguala, 37
Plaza Tapatío, 51
Popocatépetl, 12–13
Population, 11, 19, 32, 41–42, 56, 63
Precipitation, 10, 16
Presidents, 38–41, 53
Puerto Vallarta, 62
Pyramids, 26, 28–30, 34
Quetzalcóatl, 28, 31–32
Railroads, 17, 38, 40
Religion, 24–26, 28, 34–35, 50–52
Republic of Mexico, federal, 7, 10, 37
Rio Grande, 10, 13

Rivera, Diego, 4, 30, 36, 52–53
Rivers, 10, 13, 16, 57
Roads, 8, 39–40
Roman Catholic Church, 26, 34–35, 38, 40
Santa Anna, Antonio, López de, 37–38
Sierra Madre del Sur, 12, 17
Sierra Madre Occidental, 11, 17–18, 57
Sierra Madre Oriental, 11, 14, 17
Sinaloa (state), 57
Sisal, 54–55
Slaves, 34–35, 58
Sonora (state), 46, 57
Spain, 7–8, 12, 21, 24–25, 30–36, 43, 50, 58
Sports, 4, 8–9, 25
Sugar, 54, 57
Supreme Court of Justice, 41
Tabasco (state), 21, 56
Tamiahua, Lake of, 13
Taxco, 18
Tehuantepec, Isthmus of, 12, 16
Tenochtitlán, 30–34
Teotihuacán, 20, 26, 28–29
Texas, 38, 57
Textiles, 42, 48, 51, 61
Tijuana, 62
Tlatelolco, 30
Tlaxcalans, 33–34
Toltecs, 8, 31
Totonacs, 45
Tourism, 5, 8, 47, 62
Tribes, Indian
  Aztec, 8, 12, 29–34, 37, 48
  Chichimec, 28
  Maya, 22–28, 31
  Olmec, 21–22
  Tlaxcalan, 33–34
  Toltec, 8, 31
  Totonac, 45
  Yaqui, 46
  Zapotec, 25, 38
Tula, 8, 19
Underdeveloped areas, 12, 17
United States, 10, 13, 17, 38–41, 48, 50, 52, 57, 59–63
University City, 4, 53
Urbanization, 42, 54, 63
Uxmal, 24
Velázquez, Diego, 32
Veracruz (city), 15, 22, 29, 32, 60
Veracruz (state), 13, 45, 54
Victoria, Manuel Félix, Fernández (Guadalupe), 37
Villa, Francisco (Pancho), 40
Volcanoes, 8, 12–13
Wheat, 17, 54, 57
World War II, 40, 61
Xochimilco, 62
Yaquis, 46
Yucatán Peninsula, 10, 12, 15–16, 24, 28, 55
Zapata, Emiliano, 40
Zapotecs, 25, 38
Zócalo, 5, 39